At The Mall

By Pat Birtwistle

Illustrations by Bradley Moore
Original Cover Drawing by Antonio Montana Morales

Patnor Publishing

ACKNOWLEDGMENTS

A heartfelt thanks to Pat Nelson (my friend and research consultant) for her help and encouragement, Nick Sidoti for his enthusiasm, wealth of ideas and insights; Ann Marie Crocco for allowing the students in her school to pilot these novelettes, Angela Marcov who piloted these novelettes and showed such enthusiasm, and to Carole McGregor and Judy Metler for their editing skills. And a special thanks to Paul Dayboll, Linda Roote and Bradley Moore for their help with how to best get these books printed and for creating our website.

Above all, a very special thanks to Norm, my husband and best friend, for all his hard work in making these books become a reality.

At The Mall

By Pat Birtwistle

Illustrations by Bradley Moore
Original Cover Drawing by Antonio Montana Morales

At The Mall

CHAPTER 1

Money

This was it! Summer was coming to an end, and the kids had to get things for school. They had money and were going to the mall to get their stuff.

"You just get what you have to," said Bob's mom. "And see if you can stay out of trouble at the mall. You may get lunch there if you have time. Be back by two. We have some things we should do before you go back to school."

The kids went to the mall a few times. They did not have a lot of money, so they did not go over there much. This day, they all had money to get their stuff.

"This should be fun!" said Beth on the way. "If we can get good stuff and have money left, we can get lunch and maybe some CDs."

"Can we get things with the leftover money or should we take it home?" asked Dan.

"Mom didn't say to bring the money back, so she must think we will not have much left. I think we can get stuff we want," Nick said. "By the time we get the things we have to get, there will not be much money left. But let's see how we do!" said Dan.

The rest of the kids said that Kim's plan was a good one. Maybe they could pool their money at the end and get something that they all wanted.

When they got to the mall, they all went to get their school things.

"How much money do you have left?" asked Nick as they left the shop.

"We still have lots, but we have to get some things to wear," the girls said.

"We do too," said Dan. "If we get going, we could get it all by noon."

So, the girls took off to get their things. The boys did not have as much to get, so they went slowly into the shops.

Kim was by one of the shops when she saw a dirty old bag. She gave it a kick. She could tell that there was something in it. She picked it up and opened it. The bag had a lot money in it. She wanted to yell out, "I'm rich." But she just took it over to Beth. She could not keep her hand still as she opened of the bag for Beth.

"Look!" she said.

"Wow!" Beth said when she looked into the bag. "Where did you find that?"

"It was over there by the door. I picked it up. There is no one over there looking for it. I don't see anyone."

Kim went back to the door and looked at the folks passing by. No one stopped. They all kept going by her.

Then she went back to Beth and said, "Let's get out of here. I'm rich!"

"Let's just get the things we want and we'll see what the boys think you should do," said Beth.

"What? No way!" said Kim. She wanted to keep the money. She was upset with Beth, but she did what Beth said. She got her things.

It was noon when they had all their stuff. Kim saw the boys by the food stand. She came over to them with the bag in her hand.

"Don't tell us you got into some more trouble, Kim," said Nick. He could tell that something was up by looking at her.

"No! No! Look at this! I picked it up, and there was all this money in it. No one was looking for it, so I kept it."

"Wow! How much is in there?" asked Bob.

"A lot!" Kim said.

"Let's have lunch. We have lots of time before we have to go home. We'll have to think of what you should do with it," said Dan.

"I don't want food," Kim said. "I just want to take this money home."

Beth said, "Look, Kim, it is not as if it is just a little money. You cannot take it home. Someone must be looking for it."

"But," Bob said, "she did find it. She should not have to give it up. Finders, keepers!"

"Someone must be looking for it," Dan said.

"I think so too!" said Beth.

"It's not yours, Kim. You have to try to find out who lost it," said Nick. "If you can find them, they may give you some of it. But you can't just keep it."

"I did find it so I can keep it," Kim said. She was getting mad now. She did not think that the kids should tell her what to do with the money. It was not their money. They should just keep out of it. They were making her feel badly about it.

CHAPTER 2

The Best Thing To Do

Lunch was over, and Kim still did not have a plan. As last she said, "O.K., I'll take it to the shop where I picked it up. I just don't want to do that, but I will. I'll be back." She left for the shop. She was still upset.

The rest of the kids went to look for CDs. They still had money left. They were thinking that they should take the rest of their money home, but their folks did not tell them to. If they could find the CDs that they wanted, they would get them.

Kim went into the shop and asked for the boss. She told him that she had some money that someone had lost. She let him look into the bag at all that money.

"So why are you telling me?" asked the man.

"Someone must be looking for the money," said Kim. "I wanted to take it home, but the kids told me we should try to find out who lost it."

"Tell you what!" said the man. "If you left the money here, and no one comes looking for it by the end of the day, it is yours. How's that?" he asked.

"I like that," Kim said and she gave the bag of money to the man. "What time should I come back?" she asked.

"Come back just before five," said the man.

As she left the shop, Kim saw a man standing by the door. He gave her an odd look. He was a big man and Kim could not think of why he would be looking at her. She did not like the way he looked. She felt funny when she saw him and went, almost running, back to the kids. Kim told the kids that she had left the money at the shop. Then she said, "There was a man standing by the shop when I left there. He kept looking at me. Do you think that the money is his?" she asked. "Maybe that is why he was looking at me like that."

"Do you see him now?" Bob asked.

Kim looked at all the men going by them in the mall.

"I don't see him," Kim said. "Maybe it was just me. All that money is getting to me."

"We should get going," said Beth. "It is after two, and we are in trouble. We were told to be home by now."

As the kids left the mall, Kim saw the man again. He was looking at the kids. "There he is! That's him!" she told the kids. "If the money is his, why didn't he just ask the man at the shop? Why is he coming after us?"

"Wow, he is big. I cannot see what he looks like from here." Nick said. "Should we try going over there to get a look?"

"Let's not," Dan said. "Kim did not see him when she came back. He could just be going home too. He is not looking this way. Let's just get out of here."

So the kids set out for home. When they slowed down, Dan looked back. He could see the man. He was way back, but it was him. Dan did not tell the kids what he saw. He did not want to upset them. He began running and yelled at Nick, "Come on. You are so slow. I'll get home before you do." He kept looking back as he ran. The man was still there.

When they got to the block, Dan told Nick what he had seen. Nick took a look back but he could not see the man.

"Maybe it wasn't him," Nick said.

Dan said, "It was him. He was big and wearing all black like the man Kim saw. Why do you think he is coming after her?"

"Do you think he is coming after Kim?" Nick asked. "Or, do you think the money is his?"

"It can't be his. He would be at the shop looking for it. I don't like this," Dan said. "He is not from here, so why is he coming this way?"

Nick said, "Maybe we should get Beth's mom. The cops should help us out."

"But, if we do that, our folks will think that we went looking for trouble again," said Bob. "I think we can do this without their help."

"Let's just take this one step at a time. Maybe that man is not after Kim or the money," said Dan.

CHAPTER 3
The Man

The two boys did not want to tell Kim, so they just went home. They were in trouble again. This time, because they were late. Nick and Dan said they would go to the big rock by the swamp if their folks would let them out of the house. By now, the kids' moms had made a pact, too. School would begin soon, so they would not get mad at their kids.

They wanted the kids back in school, and they wanted the last days of summer to be good ones.

The kids had been in so much trouble that summer. Nick gave his mom the rest of his money. She looked at the stuff he got. She told him that he did a good job getting the school things and still had money left. He told his mom about Kim's money, but he did not tell her about the man. Then Nick went to get Bob.

On the way to the rock, Nick told Bob that Dan had seen the man when they were coming home. They had to keep a look out for Kim and the money if she got it back. But if the man just wanted the money, why didn't he go to the shop where Kim had left it? Why was he after her?

The boys sat on the rock and came up with a plan. They would go looking for the man. They would keep track of him. They left the rock and went on their way looking for him. Nick went to Kim's house and Bob took the path back to the mall. They said that they would all go to Kim's house to take her back to the mall on time.

Bob and Dan did not find the man but Nick spotted him just down the block from Kim's house. The man saw him too. The man began to run. Nick took off after him. The man was fast but so was Nick. The man ran behind some trees. Nick just saw his back when he did that. As Nick got to that spot, he saw the man duck behind some bushes. By the time Nick got to the bushes, the man was not there.

Nick took a good look, but he had lost him. There were some tracks where the man had run. But there were lots of tracks and Nick could not tell which ones were the man's.

"Now what?" Nick asked himself. "Do I try to find him or do I go and get Dan and Bob to help me? If I do see him, what should I do? I could ask him why he is here on this block. If he got away, maybe he will just not come back." Nick was just going to head back to Kim's house.

In a flash someone grabbed Nick from behind. Before Nick could think, he was back behind the bushes. He could not tell who had grabbed him. He did not have time to think.

"I want that money. What do you think you can do?" asked a man from behind him. "Think you are a big man, do you? Think you can stop me, do you? I'm telling you now. Back off! Go home! Stay there or you'll find out what trouble is!"

The man just pushed Nick down so fast that Nick was winded and could not get up. He lay there for a time. When he could stand and look for who it was, the man had left. Nick went slowly back down the block. He kept a look out for the man. He had to tell the kids that the man was after the money. He would have to tell them what the man said. He had not hurt Nick as much as he could have. Nick was thinking that the man could have killed him on the spot. He had to let the other kids in on this.

Kim wanted that money but so did that man. If she went to get it and the kids went with her, they would be in a lot more trouble than they had been in all summer.

As Nick was getting to Kim's house, he spotted the man again. He was down the block from Kim's. He was standing by a tree looking at the kids on the steps. The kids were waving at Nick as he came down the block. They were having a good time. They had not seen the man. The tree had hidden him. Nick was getting more and more upset. He could not think of what he should do.

CHAPTER 4

Should We Go Back?

Nick did not let on that he had seen the man. He put his head down and went up the steps. The kids were having such a good time that he did not want to upset them. Nick sat down next to the boys. Kim said that her mom had told her that she could have the money if it was still at the shop at five. She said if she hung onto it and put it in the bank, she would be rich at last.

The rest of the kids could think of all kinds of things she could get with all that money. They had a good time thinking of what to do with it. All but Nick that is. He did not say a thing.

Nick got up and said to Dan and Bob, "I want a pop. Let's go to my house and get one. We'll be back."

"You can get a pop here," Kim said. "I'll pay."

"That's funny," said Nick. "I want to show these two something. We'll be back well before five. We'll get you to the mall on time." The girls did not stop to think of why he left. They kept on talking of what to do with the money.

They were going slowly down the block as Nick told Bob and Dan that the man was still on the block. "I saw him a few houses over from Kim's. He is behind a tree." He told them that the man had grabbed him and told him to back off. "He is after Kim and the money." The boys did not say a thing when Nick told them the man had grabbed him.

"He could have hurt me, but he didn't. I did not see what he looked like. He stayed behind me," Nick said. "We should tell Kim. She should not try to get that money back. This is not funny. It's the biggest mess we have had all summer. This time someone could get killed. If we try to help her get that money, it could be bad for all of us."

When they got to Nick's house, Nick went and got the pop. They sat down and began thinking of ways to help Kim get the money and get rid of the man. They did not want the cops in on this. If they went to the cops, their folks would get upset again. They did not want that.

"He's too big for us to take on. He could pick the three of us up and pitch us like sticks. We are running out of time, and I can't think of a thing we can do. Kim will not let that money go," Nick told them. "She wants to be rich."

By now it was four, so they had to get back to Kim's. They did not want her and Beth going to the mall before they got back.

They wanted to see if the man was still there, behind the tree. If the girls stayed at Kim's house, he would not hurt them.

"I think we should tell Kim. If she wants that money that badly, she will have to go and get it by herself. Then it is up to her if she gets hurt," Bob said. "I think the man will just take the money and not hurt her."

"OK," said Nick. "Let's go back and tell her. Then it's up to her."

"We can't do that! I think we should just tell Kim that we went to the mall and that someone had come for the money. That way she will not go back," said Dan. "If she thinks someone came for the money, she will be hurt, but she will be out of trouble."

"I like that," Nick said. "Let's not go back to Kim's too fast. Let's stay here and let her think we went to the mall. If we take our time getting back, maybe she will not go back for the money."

So the boys stayed at Nick's house. They kept looking at the time. They wanted to time this so that they could stop Kim from going to the mall. But they would find out that Kim and Beth had left for the mall because they could not stand it. Kim wanted to be there before five, so they left a little after four, without the boys.

CHAPTER 5

Back At The Mall

As the boys came down the block, they kept a look out for the man. "He was behind that tree over there. He's not there now. Maybe he left thinking we were not going back for the money," said Nick.

"If he left, then we can take Kim back to the mall. She will get her money after all," Bob said.

The boys were thinking that they had a good plan. When they left Nick's house, they took their time getting back to Kim's. When they got to Kim's, they saw that the girls were not on the steps.

"Oh, no!" said Bob. "You don't think they left without us, do you? They would not do that, would they? They must just be in the house. Let them just be in the house!"

They came running up the steps. They yelled for Kim's Mom. She came out of the house and said, "I told them to stay here till you boys got back. That Kim and her money! They wanted to be at the mall in lots of time. So, they left."

Nick kept looking back. He wanted to see if the man was still there. Nick could not see him, so he must have left. Nick was thinking, "The man went after the girls." They had to stop him before he hurt them. They took off running for the mall. They did not have time to tell Kim's Mom what trouble Kim could be in. As they took off running, Kim's Mom was standing on the steps saying, "Oh no! Oh no! Not more trouble!"

The boys kept running all the way to the mall. When they got to the mall, they did not see the girls. They wished they had asked Kim where she had left the money. They had to keep looking.

"They went this way when they left us. It has to be this way. Come on!" Dan said. "Where are you two? Why didn't you tell us which shop you were in? Why didn't we ask? Where are you?"

After a time, Dan spotted them.

"There they are! Over there. Slow down! Nick, do you see that man?" asked Bob. "Take a good look. Is he in the mall?"

The boys stopped so that Nick could try to find the man. A little time went by. Then Nick said, "I don't see him, but he could be here somewhere. Should we stay back? We could help the girls if he thinks that we are not here."

"Good thinking," said Bob. "It is just before five, so Kim will be trying to get the money soon."

Kim was just going into the shop when Nick saw the man come over from the food stands. Kim did not see him because she was thinking of the money. The man went to the door of a shop at the end of the mall. He kept looking at the shop that Kim went into.

"What are we going to do?" asked Dan.

Kim came out of the shop with the bag of money. She and Beth were making their way down the mall when the man came up behind them. He pushed Beth away. He grabbed for the bag of money but Kim began running.

Beth was down, but she was not hurt. She was looking at the man running after Kim.

Two cops stepped out of a doorway. They stopped the man. They led him out of the mall. They had seen the man push Beth and grab for the money.

Soon, the kids' folks were all at the mall too. When the boys took off running for the mall, Kim's mom had asked the cops to find out what trouble the kids were in this time. Then she went to get the kids' folks. She told them that she felt that the kids were in trouble again.

"It's a good thing school is about to begin," said the folks. "We cannot take much more trouble!"

NEW START SUSPENSE SERIES
BY PATRICIA BIRTWISTLE

THE SWAMP

THE OLD HOUSE

WHAT A DAY

THE JUNKYARD

THE TRIP

AT THE MALL

At The Mall

The kids must get their stuff for school. They split up so that they can get all their things and then have lunch. Kim, the one who wants to get rich, finds a bag of money and wants to keep it. The rest of the kids tell her that she should not keep it. Someone must be looking for it. Kim takes the bag of money to try to get it back to the one who lost it. Someone has seen Kim with the money. Trouble begins again for the kids.

"This book is amazingly interesting. Right from the first chapter it gets your attention."
-Mary Kate

"This book is really really good. It gets exciting when the girls go to the mall alone."
-Jamie

ISBN 0-9733663-6-2